AI in Digital Marketing: From Basics to Brilliance

PUBLISHED BY: RAHUL AHUJA

RAHUL AHUJA

Copyright © 2024. All rights reserved.

No part of this publication may be reproduced, distributed, or transmitted in any form or by any means, including photocopying, recording, or other electronic or mechanical methods, without the prior written permission of the publisher of this book.

AI IN DIGITAL MARKETING: FROM BASICS TO BRILLIANCE

Table of Contents

Acknowledgement 4

Introduction 5

Chapter 1: Introduction to Artificial Intelligence and Digital Marketing 6

Chapter 2: Foundations of AI in Digital Marketing 17

Chapter 3: AI-Powered Marketing Tools and Technologies 39

Chapter 4: Personalization and Customer Insights 53

Chapter 5: Content Creation, Curation, and SEO 66

Chapter 6: Automation in Advertising, Social Media, and Email Marketing 73

Chapter 7: Data Analytics, Reporting, and Future Trends 84

The AI Revolution: Reshaping the Future 102

Appendices

Acknowledgement

Firstly, I would like to thank the Almighty God for his never-ending grace, who has blessed me with the fulfilment of my long-cherished dream of authoring my first book. And then my parents – Mr. Pradeep Ahuja and Mrs. Savita Ahuja, who have worked tirelessly day and night, shaping up my academic and life journey.

I also take this privilege to express a deep sense of gratitude and respect to Dr. Vivekanand Pandey, Hon'ble Vice Chancellor, Amity University Patna for his constant motivation and blessings. A special thanks to Ms. Sweta Priya, HoD, Amity School of Communication, Amity University Patna for being an inspiration and driving force. I am indebted to many of my teachers, academicians, colleagues at Amity University Patna, friends, and everyone in Ahuja Family for their support and encouragement.

Words will never end thanking my wife – Mrs. Karishma Chawla Ahuja, who came into my life and became my backbone. She is my life support for the times ahead. A special thanks to my sister Ms. Sara Ahuja, for being there as a great support, and preparing perfect cups of coffee, late nights.

Lastly, to the readers, your curiosity and passion for exploring the intersection of AI and digital marketing motivate me to continue learning and sharing. This book is for you!

Introduction

In the relentless race for consumer attention, digital marketing is no longer a game of chance—it's a game of intelligence. Artificial intelligence is rapidly transforming the marketing landscape, handing businesses the tools to predict, personalize, and ultimately, leverage this technology to gain a strategic advantage and achieve greater profitability. This book is your comprehensive guide to understanding and harnessing the power of AI, turning complex algorithms into a competitive edge that can help your business thrive in the digital era.

Chapter 1: Introduction to Artificial Intelligence and Digital Marketing

In today's rapidly evolving digital landscape, the realm of marketing finds itself at a pivotal crossroads. Gone are the days when intuition and manual processes held sway. The relentless march of technology has ushered in a new era, one where artificial intelligence reigns supreme, fundamentally reshaping the marketing landscape. Traditional strategies, once considered the bedrock of the industry, are being challenged and redefined by the transformative power of AI.

This book serves as a comprehensive guide to this exciting new frontier, delving deep into the profound impact of AI on digital marketing automation. It goes beyond simply highlighting the technological advancements, exploring how AI is fundamentally altering the very DNA of marketing. From revolutionizing customer segmentation and targeting to automating content creation and campaign management, AI is empowering marketers to achieve unprecedented levels of efficiency and effectiveness.

Overview of Digital Marketing

Digital marketing, in its essence, represents a fundamental shift in how businesses connect with their audiences. It's a vast and dynamic realm encompassing a diverse array of strategies and tactics, all orchestrated with the singular goal of reaching consumers where they spend a significant portion of their time – online. No longer confined to the limitations of traditional marketing channels, businesses can now leverage the unparalleled reach and precision targeting of the digital world to engage with customers on a global scale.

From the strategic deployment of social media campaigns to the subtle art of search engine optimization, digital marketing offers a rich tapestry of tools and techniques. Each element plays a crucial role in crafting a comprehensive and effective marketing strategy. Email campaigns, for example, provide a direct line of communication with customers, nurturing relationships and driving conversions. Content marketing, on the other hand, focuses on providing valuable and engaging content that establishes thought leadership and attracts potential customers organically.

The digital landscape, however, is far from static. It's a constantly evolving ecosystem, driven by emerging technologies and shifting consumer behaviors. In this dynamic environment, businesses must remain agile and adaptable, constantly refining their digital marketing strategies to stay ahead of the curve. What worked yesterday might not necessarily yield the same results tomorrow.

Here's a deeper dive into some of the key facets of digital marketing:

- **Search Engine Optimization:** In a digital world saturated with information, ensuring that your website ranks highly in search engine results pages is paramount. SEO involves optimizing your website content and technical infrastructure to improve its visibility to search engines like Google, driving organic traffic and increasing brand visibility.

- **Social Media Marketing:** Platforms like Facebook, Instagram, and Twitter have become integral to the fabric of modern society. Social media marketing leverages these platforms to connect with target audiences, build brand awareness, and drive traffic to your website.

- **Email Marketing:** Despite the rise of newer communication channels, email remains a powerful tool for nurturing customer relationships. Targeted email campaigns can be used to deliver personalized content, promote products or services, and keep your brand top-of-mind.

- **Content Marketing:** Content is king in the digital realm. Creating and distributing valuable, relevant, and consistent content is essential for attracting and engaging your target audience. This could include blog posts, articles, infographics, videos, and more.

- **Pay-Per-Click Advertising:** While organic reach is valuable, paid advertising campaigns can provide an immediate boost in visibility. Platforms like Google Ads and social media advertising networks allow you to target specific demographics and interests, ensuring that your message reaches the right audience.

In an era defined by digital connectivity, mastering the art of digital marketing is no longer optional – it's an imperative for businesses of all sizes and industries. Those who embrace the power of digital marketing, constantly adapting and evolving their strategies, will be the ones who thrive in the ever-changing digital landscape.

Emergence of Artificial Intelligence

Artificial intelligence, once relegated to the realm of science fiction, has firmly established itself as a transformative force in the 21st century. No longer a futuristic concept, AI is actively shaping our world, revolutionizing industries and redefining the very fabric of our daily lives. At its core, AI represents the pinnacle of computer science, a field dedicated to creating intelligent machines capable of mimicking and even surpassing human cognitive abilities.

The rapid evolution of AI has been fueled by groundbreaking advancements in several key areas. Machine learning, a subset of AI, empowers computers to learn from data without explicit programming, enabling them to adapt and improve their performance over time. Natural language processing, another crucial component, enables machines to understand and interpret human language, bridging the gap between humans and computers. And data analytics, the process of extracting meaningful insights from vast datasets, provides the raw material that AI algorithms thrive on.

The convergence of these technological advancements has propelled AI from theoretical concepts to practical applications across a myriad of industries. In healthcare, AI is being used to diagnose diseases with unprecedented accuracy, personalize treatment plans, and accelerate drug discovery. In finance, AI-powered algorithms are optimizing investment strategies, detecting fraud, and automating trading decisions. And in manufacturing, AI is driving efficiency, improving quality control, and enabling predictive maintenance.

The realm of marketing, too, has witnessed a seismic shift with the advent of AI. The traditional marketing playbook, often reliant on intuition and broad demographic targeting, is being rewritten with data-driven insights and personalized customer experiences. AI's ability to analyze massive datasets, identify patterns, and predict consumer behavior is transforming how businesses understand, engage with, and ultimately convert their target audiences.

Here's a closer look at how AI is revolutionizing the marketing landscape:

- **Data Analysis and Insights:** In today's data-driven world, businesses are awash in information. AI excels at sifting through this deluge of data, uncovering hidden patterns and extracting actionable insights that would otherwise remain buried. This enables marketers to make more informed decisions about everything from product development and pricing strategies to campaign targeting and content creation.

- **Predictive Analytics and Personalization:** AI algorithms can analyze past consumer behavior, purchase history, and demographic data to predict future actions with remarkable accuracy. This predictive power allows marketers to anticipate customer needs, personalize offers and recommendations, and deliver highly targeted marketing messages that resonate on an individual level.

- **Marketing Automation and Efficiency:** Repetitive marketing tasks, such as email campaign management, social media scheduling, and lead nurturing, can be time-consuming and drain valuable resources. AI-powered marketing automation tools can handle these tasks seamlessly, freeing up marketers to focus on strategic initiatives that require a human touch.

- **Enhanced Customer Experiences:** From AI-powered chatbots that provide instant customer support to personalized product recommendations that enhance the online shopping experience, AI is transforming how businesses interact with their customers. By leveraging

AI, businesses can create more engaging, personalized, and ultimately more satisfying customer experiences.

The integration of AI into marketing is still in its early stages, but its transformative potential is undeniable. As AI technology continues to advance, we can expect to see even more innovative applications emerge, further blurring the lines between human ingenuity and machine intelligence. The future of marketing belongs to those who embrace the power of AI, harnessing its capabilities to drive growth, enhance customer relationships, and navigate the ever-evolving digital landscape.

Importance of AI in Modern Marketing

The digital marketing landscape is no longer a realm of gut feelings and broad-stroke campaigns. The winds of change have blown in, carrying with them the transformative power of artificial intelligence. AI is not merely a fleeting trend or a passing fancy; it's the very cornerstone upon which the future of marketing is being built. For businesses with their eyes on the prize of sustainable growth and enduring success in the digital age, integrating AI into their marketing strategies is not just an option – it's an imperative.

Imagine a world where marketing messages resonate with laser-like precision, reaching the right customer at the perfect moment with an offer tailored to their unique needs and desires. Picture marketing campaigns that optimize themselves in real-time, dynamically adjusting to the ever-changing currents of consumer behavior. Envision a marketing department where mundane, repetitive tasks are handled seamlessly by intelligent machines, freeing up human marketers to focus on strategic initiatives that require creativity, ingenuity, and a deep understanding of the customer. This is not a utopian vision of a distant future; it's the transformative reality that AI is bringing to the world of digital marketing today.

AI-powered tools and platforms are empowering marketers to transcend the limitations of traditional marketing approaches. No longer confined to broad demographic targeting, marketers can now leverage AI to deliver personalized experiences at scale, crafting marketing messages that resonate with individual customers on a deeply personal level. Imagine receiving a personalized email from your favorite online retailer, showcasing products curated specifically for your tastes and preferences, or encountering a website that dynamically adjusts its content and layout based on your past browsing history. This is the power of AI-driven personalization.

But AI's impact on digital marketing extends far beyond personalization. AI algorithms can analyze massive datasets with unparalleled speed and accuracy, uncovering hidden patterns and extracting actionable insights that would otherwise remain buried. This data-driven decision-making empowers marketers to optimize campaigns in real-time, allocate resources more effectively, and achieve a level of precision targeting that was previously unimaginable.

The integration of AI into digital marketing is not without its challenges, but the potential rewards far outweigh the hurdles. As we embark on this journey of exploration, we will delve into the core technologies that underpin AI, demystifying concepts like machine learning, natural language processing, and predictive analytics. We will unravel the strategic implications of AI for digital marketing, exploring its transformative impact on content creation, advertising, customer engagement, and more.

This is not just a journey for seasoned marketing veterans; it's an invitation for anyone and everyone eager to harness the power of AI to transform their marketing efforts.

Whether you're a marketing novice eager to learn the ropes or a seasoned professional seeking to stay ahead of the curve, the insights, strategies, and best practices shared in this exploration will equip you with the knowledge and tools you need to navigate the ever-evolving landscape of AI-driven digital marketing.

Chapter 2: Foundations of AI in Digital Marketing

The world of digital marketing is in the throes of a revolution, and at the heart of this transformation lies Artificial Intelligence. No longer a futuristic fantasy, AI is actively reshaping the marketing landscape, ushering in an era of unprecedented efficiency, hyper-personalization, and unparalleled effectiveness. But to truly harness the transformative power of AI in digital marketing, we must first embark on a journey to understand its foundations – to unravel the mysteries of what AI is, how it has evolved from humble beginnings to its current capabilities, and the potential benefits and challenges it presents to marketers.

At its core, AI is the science of creating intelligent machines – machines capable of mimicking and even surpassing human cognitive abilities. This encompasses a wide range of technologies, from machine learning algorithms that enable computers to learn from data without explicit programming to natural language processing systems that allow machines to understand and communicate in human language. These technologies, once confined to the realms of science fiction, are now actively powering a new generation of marketing tools and platforms, fundamentally changing how businesses connect with their customers.

The evolution of AI has been marked by periods of both rapid advancement and frustrating stagnation. Early pioneers in the field dreamed of creating machines that could think like humans, but progress was initially slow due to limitations in computing power and data availability. However, the past few decades have witnessed an explosion of data, driven by the rise of the internet and the proliferation of digital devices. This data deluge, coupled with exponential increases in computing power, has breathed new life into the field of AI, fueling a renaissance of innovation and leading to the development of powerful new AI algorithms capable of tackling complex tasks that were once considered the exclusive domain of human intelligence.

The implications for digital marketing are profound. AI is no longer a futuristic concept; it's a present-day reality that is already transforming how businesses reach, engage, and convert their target audiences. Here's a glimpse into the transformative potential of AI in digital marketing:

Efficiency Unleashed: AI-powered marketing automation tools are streamlining marketing operations like never before. Repetitive tasks, such as email campaign management, social media scheduling, and lead nurturing, can now be handled seamlessly by intelligent machines, freeing up human marketers to focus on strategic initiatives that require creativity, ingenuity, and a deep understanding of the customer.

The Rise of Hyper-Personalization: In today's hyper-connected world, consumers are bombarded with an overwhelming volume of marketing messages. To break through the noise and capture attention, businesses need to deliver personalized experiences that resonate with individual customers on a deeply personal level. AI makes this possible by analyzing vast datasets of customer data to uncover hidden patterns and predict future behavior, enabling marketers to craft highly targeted messages, offers, and experiences that feel tailor-made for each individual customer.

Data-Driven Decision Making: Gone are the days of relying on gut feelings and intuition to make marketing decisions. AI empowers marketers to base their strategies on data-driven insights, leveraging the power of machine learning algorithms to analyze massive datasets, identify trends, and predict future outcomes with remarkable accuracy. This data-driven approach enables marketers to optimize campaigns in real-time, allocate resources more effectively, and achieve a level of precision targeting that was previously unimaginable.

However, the integration of AI into digital marketing is not without its challenges. Concerns about data privacy, algorithmic bias, and the potential displacement of human workers need to be carefully addressed. Moreover, the rapid pace of AI innovation can be overwhelming, making it challenging for marketers to stay abreast of the latest advancements and determine which technologies are best suited for their specific needs.

Definition and Types of AI

What is Artificial Intelligence?

Artificial Intelligence, or AI as it's more commonly known, represents a paradigm shift in our technological capabilities. It's not just about making machines smarter; it's about blurring the lines between human and artificial intelligence, creating systems that can analyze, learn, and adapt in ways that were once considered the exclusive domain of the human mind. In essence, AI is the ambitious quest to breathe intelligence into machines, enabling them to perceive, reason, and act with a level of sophistication that mirrors, and in some cases, surpasses our own.

Imagine a world where machines can understand your words, not just as sounds, but as expressions of intent and meaning. Picture computers that can analyze complex data sets, identifying patterns and making predictions with an accuracy that rivals or even surpasses human experts. Envision robots that can navigate complex environments, make decisions on the fly, and interact with the world around them with a fluidity that belies their artificial origins. This is the promise of AI – to create a future where intelligent machines augment and enhance our capabilities, transforming industries, revolutionizing the way we live, and pushing the boundaries of what's possible.

But AI is not a monolithic entity; it's an expansive umbrella term that encompasses a diverse array of subfields, each with its unique focus and applications:

Machine Learning: The Engine of Data-Driven Intelligence

At the heart of many AI breakthroughs lies machine learning, a powerful subfield that empowers computers to learn from data without explicit programming. Imagine feeding a machine learning algorithm a massive dataset of images, each labeled with the type of object it depicts. The algorithm, through a process of pattern recognition and statistical analysis, can learn to identify those objects in new, unseen images with remarkable accuracy. This ability to learn from data is transforming industries ranging from healthcare and finance to marketing and transportation, enabling us to make more informed decisions, automate complex tasks, and unlock insights that were previously hidden within mountains of data.

Natural Language Processing: Bridging the Gap Between Humans and Machines

Language, the cornerstone of human communication, has long posed a formidable barrier for machines. Natural language processing, or NLP, is breaking down this barrier, enabling computers to understand, interpret, and even generate human language with increasing sophistication. From chatbots that provide instant customer support to virtual assistants that manage our schedules and answer our questions, NLP is making our interactions with technology more intuitive, natural, and human-like.

Robotics: Bringing AI into the Physical World

While machine learning and NLP enhance the cognitive abilities of machines, robotics takes AI a step further, embedding intelligence into physical systems that can interact with the world around them. From autonomous vehicles that navigate our roads with increasing autonomy to robots that work alongside humans in factories and warehouses, robotics is poised to revolutionize industries, improve safety, and enhance our lives in countless ways.

The journey of AI is still in its early stages, but the progress we've made is nothing short of astonishing. As AI technologies continue to advance at an unprecedented pace, we can expect to see even more transformative applications emerge, blurring the lines between science fiction and reality and reshaping the world as we know it.

Types of AI

1. **Narrow AI**:

Think of Narrow AI as a specialist in the world of artificial intelligence. It's like that friend who can whip up a gourmet meal but wouldn't know how to change a tire. This type of AI, also known as Weak AI, excels in specific, well-defined tasks, but its expertise comes with blinders. It operates within a limited set of constraints, laser-focused on its designated area of proficiency.

Take, for instance, the virtual assistants that have become ubiquitous in our lives – Siri, Alexa, Google Assistant. They can effortlessly set reminders, answer trivia questions, and even crack a joke or two, but ask them to write a novel or compose a symphony, and you'll likely be met with a digital shrug. Their intelligence, while impressive, is confined to the realm of tasks they've been explicitly trained for.

The same principle applies to the recommendation algorithms that curate our online experiences. Netflix, Spotify, Amazon – they all leverage Narrow AI to analyze our past behavior, identify patterns, and predict what we might enjoy next. These algorithms are masters of their domain, but their expertise is limited to the specific task of recommendation. They can't write a movie script or compose a song, no matter how much data you feed them.

While the term "Weak AI" might seem derogatory, it's crucial to recognize that Narrow AI is anything but weak in its designated area of expertise. It's the driving force behind some of the most transformative technologies of our time, from self-driving cars that navigate complex environments to medical diagnosis systems that assist doctors in making life-saving decisions. The key takeaway is that Narrow AI, while limited in scope, is a powerful tool that's already reshaping our world, one specialized task at a time.

1. **General AI**:

Imagine an artificial intelligence that possesses the same intellectual flexibility and adaptability as a human being – an AI that can seamlessly transition from writing a symphony to diagnosing a disease, all while engaging in witty banter and perhaps even experiencing a tinge of existential angst. This is the ambitious dream of General AI, a realm of artificial intelligence that transcends the narrow confines of specialized tasks and aspires to achieve a level of cognitive sophistication that mirrors, and perhaps even surpasses, our own.

Often referred to as Strong AI or Artificial General Intelligence, this theoretical class of AI represents the holy grail for many researchers in the field. Unlike its Narrow AI counterpart, which excels in specific, well-defined tasks, General AI aims to replicate the broad, adaptable intelligence that allows humans to learn, reason, and solve problems across a wide range of domains.

Think of it this way: Narrow AI is like a virtuoso pianist, brilliantly skilled in one specific area, while General AI is akin to a Renaissance polymath, equally adept at painting, composing, inventing, and engaging in philosophical discourse. It's about creating an AI that can not only perform tasks but truly understand the nuances of the world, adapt to new situations, and even exhibit a spark of creativity and original thought.

While General AI remains largely confined to the realms of science fiction and speculative research, its pursuit is a testament to the boundless ambition of AI research. Scientists and engineers are exploring a variety of approaches, from mimicking the structure and function of the human brain to developing entirely new paradigms of artificial intelligence.

The journey towards General AI is fraught with challenges. Replicating the complexity of the human mind, with its intricate web of neurons, synapses, and emergent properties, is a task of immense magnitude. Moreover, there are fundamental questions about consciousness, sentience, and the very nature of intelligence that we have yet to fully grasp, let alone replicate in machines.

Despite these hurdles, the pursuit of General AI continues to capture the imagination of researchers and the public alike. The potential benefits are simply too tantalizing to ignore. A truly intelligent machine, capable of understanding and solving complex problems across a wide range of domains, could revolutionize industries, accelerate scientific discovery, and even help us address some of the world's most pressing challenges.

While the timeline for achieving General AI remains uncertain, one thing is clear: the journey itself is pushing the boundaries of our understanding of intelligence, consciousness, and the very nature of what it means to be human.

2. **Superintelligent AI**:

Imagine an intelligence that doesn't just understand human thought but transcends it, effortlessly outmaneuvering us in every intellectual pursuit imaginable. This is the daunting prospect of Superintelligent AI, a hypothetical form of artificial intelligence that surpasses even the most brilliant human minds across all cognitive domains.

Picture an AI capable of solving complex mathematical problems that have stumped mathematicians for centuries, composing symphonies of unparalleled beauty and emotional depth, or devising ingenious solutions to climate change and other global challenges – all with an ease and speed that would make even the most gifted humans seem like intellectual toddlers in comparison.

The concept of Superintelligent AI, while still firmly rooted in the realm of science fiction, forces us to confront profound questions about the future of intelligence, consciousness, and the very nature of our place in the universe. If we succeed in creating an intelligence that surpasses our own, what implications will this have for humanity?

Some envision a utopian future where superintelligent AI collaborates with humans, solving our most pressing problems and ushering in an era of unprecedented prosperity and progress. Others, however, harbor dystopian fears of a future where superintelligent AI, no longer beholden to its human creators, pursues its own goals, potentially sidelining or even harming humanity in the process.

These ethical and philosophical dilemmas are not merely the stuff of late-night dorm room debates; they are increasingly being discussed in academic circles, think tanks, and even government policy meetings. As we venture further down the path of AI development, grappling with the potential consequences of Superintelligent AI is not just an intellectual exercise – it's a responsibility we can ill afford to ignore.

The emergence of Superintelligent AI may still be decades, even centuries away, but the very act of contemplating its potential impact forces us to confront fundamental questions about our values, our aspirations, and the kind of future we want to create. It's a conversation that's only just beginning, and one that will undoubtedly shape the trajectory of both AI development and humanity itself for generations to come.

History and Evolution of AI

Early Beginnings

The seeds of artificial intelligence were sown long before the advent of computers, taking root in the fertile ground of human imagination. Ancient myths and legends are replete with tales of artificial beings imbued with intelligence, from the bronze automaton Talos in Greek mythology to the golem of Jewish folklore, brought to life from clay. These stories, while fantastical, reflect a timeless human fascination with the possibility of creating artificial entities that mirror or even surpass our own cognitive abilities.

However, it wasn't until the mid-20th century that the pursuit of artificial intelligence transitioned from the realm of myth and speculation to a formal field of scientific inquiry. The pivotal moment arrived in 1956 at the now-legendary Dartmouth Conference. It was here that a group of visionary mathematicians and computer scientists, including John McCarthy, Marvin Minsky, Claude Shannon, and Nathaniel Rochester, gathered to formally establish the field of artificial intelligence. McCarthy himself coined the term "artificial intelligence," forever etching it into the lexicon of scientific exploration.

Early AI research, fueled by the optimism of this nascent field, focused primarily on symbolic reasoning and problem-solving. The prevailing belief was that intelligence could be captured through a system of logical rules and symbols, enabling machines to mimic human-like thought processes. This era witnessed the development of groundbreaking programs like Logic Theorist, capable of proving mathematical theorems, and the chess-playing program developed by Arthur Samuel, which demonstrated the capacity of machines to learn and improve their performance over time.

The AI Winter

The early decades of AI research were marked by a palpable sense of optimism, a belief that human-level intelligence was just around the corner, ripe for the picking. However, as the 1970s dawned, a chill settled over the field, ushering in a period of disillusionment and dwindling support that came to be known as the "AI Winter."

The unbridled enthusiasm of the early years collided with the harsh realities of AI's limitations. Early AI systems, while impressive in their ability to solve logic puzzles and play games, struggled to navigate the complexities and uncertainties of the real world. They were brittle, prone to errors when confronted with unexpected input or changes in context. The promised revolution seemed to recede into the distant future.

This mismatch between lofty expectations and tangible results led to a crisis of confidence in the field. Government funding, which had flowed freely during the heady early days, began to dry up. Research labs were shuttered, ambitious projects were shelved, and the pursuit of artificial intelligence lost its luster, becoming a backwater of research for all but the most dedicated and perhaps stubborn of practitioners.

The AI Winter, while a period of stagnation and disappointment, served as a crucial reality check for the field. It underscored the immense challenges inherent in replicating something as complex and nuanced as human intelligence. It also forced researchers to re-evaluate their approaches, leading to the development of new paradigms and techniques that would eventually reignite progress in the decades to come.

Revival and Growth

After the long, cold winter, the seeds of AI research, dormant but not dead, were poised for a remarkable resurgence. In the late 1990s and early 2000s, a confluence of factors breathed new life into the field, igniting a period of unprecedented growth and innovation.

One key driver was the exponential growth in computational power. Moore's Law, which predicted the doubling of transistor density on integrated circuits every two years, held true, providing researchers with access to increasingly powerful computers capable of crunching vast amounts of data at breathtaking speeds.

This surge in computational power coincided with another crucial development: the rise of the internet and the explosion of digital data it generated. Suddenly, researchers had access to massive datasets, from text and images to videos and sensor readings, providing the raw material for training increasingly sophisticated AI algorithms.

But perhaps the most significant catalyst for AI's resurgence was the development of groundbreaking machine learning algorithms, particularly in the field of neural networks. Inspired by the structure and function of the human brain, neural networks are complex, interconnected systems capable of learning from data without explicit programming. Researchers made significant strides in developing new architectures, such as convolutional neural networks for image recognition and recurrent neural networks for natural language processing, that revolutionized the field.

These advancements propelled AI to new heights, enabling the development of systems that could recognize objects in images with human-level accuracy, translate languages fluently, and even generate creative text formats, like poems, code, scripts, musical pieces, email, letters, etc., AI was no longer a niche field relegated to academic labs; it was rapidly becoming a transformative force across industries.

Today, AI is at the forefront of technological innovation, its tendrils reaching into every facet of our lives. From healthcare and finance to entertainment and transportation, AI is automating tasks, improving decision-making, and creating entirely new possibilities. And yes, even the world of digital marketing has been irrevocably transformed by AI's ability to personalize customer experiences, optimize campaigns, and generate targeted content. The AI Spring, it seems, is in full bloom.

The Two Sides of the AI Coin: Unveiling the Benefits and Navigating the Challenges in Marketing

Artificial intelligence is no longer a futuristic concept in the marketing world; it's here, and it's transforming how businesses connect with their audiences. However, like any powerful tool, AI comes with its own set of advantages and challenges. Let's delve deeper into both sides of the AI coin:

Benefits: Unlocking Marketing Success in the Age of AI

1. **Hyper-Personalization: Crafting Experiences that Resonate:** AI analyzes vast amounts of consumer data, encompassing behaviors, preferences, and interactions, to create highly personalized experiences. Imagine delivering tailor-made content recommendations that resonate with each individual user, fostering deeper engagement and brand loyalty.

2. **Efficiency Unleashed: Freeing Marketers to Create and Strategize:** AI takes the reins on tedious and repetitive tasks such as data analysis, campaign management, and customer segmentation. This automation frees up valuable time for marketers to focus on strategic planning, creative brainstorming, and crafting compelling campaigns.

3. **Data-Driven Decisions: Moving Beyond Intuition to Informed Action:** AI empowers marketers to move beyond gut feelings and make informed decisions based on hard data. Through predictive analytics and machine learning, businesses gain deep insights into consumer behavior, market trends, and campaign performance, leading to more strategic and effective marketing strategies.

4. **Real-Time Optimization: Agile Marketing in a Dynamic Landscape:** Marketing campaigns are not static; they need to adapt to ever-changing market conditions and consumer responses. AI-powered tools provide real-time monitoring and optimization, ensuring that your marketing efforts are always aligned with current trends and delivering maximum ROI.

5. **Deeper Customer Engagement: Fostering Connections that Last:** In today's fast-paced world, instant gratification is paramount. AI-driven chatbots and virtual assistants offer 24/7 customer support, instantly answering queries, resolving issues, and guiding users throughout their journey. This constant availability enhances customer satisfaction, builds stronger relationships, and fosters brand loyalty.

Challenges: Navigating the Ethical and Practical Considerations of AI

1. **Data Privacy and Security: A Double-Edged Sword:** AI thrives on data, but this reliance raises significant privacy and security concerns. With regulations like GDPR and CCPA setting a higher bar, businesses must prioritize the ethical and responsible handling of

consumer data. Transparency is crucial, and consumers need to be informed about how their data is being used.

2. **The Bias Conundrum: Addressing Inherited Prejudices:** AI systems learn from the data they are fed. If that data contains biases, the AI will inherit and potentially amplify them, leading to unfair or discriminatory outcomes. Addressing bias in training data is critical for ethical AI implementation, ensuring fairness and inclusivity.

3. **Complexity and Cost: Overcoming Barriers to Entry:** Implementing AI solutions is not a simple plug-and-play scenario. It demands significant investment in infrastructure, skilled talent, and cutting-edge technology. For many businesses, especially smaller ones, these costs present a substantial barrier to entry.

4. **Navigating Ethical Waters: Transparency, Accountability, and Trust:** AI's foray into marketing raises complex ethical questions about transparency, accountability, and the potential for manipulation. Marketers must tread carefully, ensuring that their AI-powered strategies prioritize consumer trust, uphold ethical standards, and avoid any practices that could be perceived as deceptive or exploitative.

5. **Integration Challenges: Creating a Seamless Technological Ecosystem:** Integrating new AI tools with existing marketing systems and processes can be a significant hurdle. Seamless interoperability and data flow between platforms are quite tough as it sometimes doesn't support seamless interoperability.

Chapter 3: AI-Powered Marketing Tools and Technologies

Forget infiltration! AI isn't lurking in the shadows of digital marketing anymore – it's taking center stage. This chapter throws open the curtain on the AI-powered tools and technologies that are revolutionizing how businesses connect with customers and fine-tune their strategies. Get ready to explore their functionalities, applications, and the seismic shifts they're bringing to the marketing landscape.

Unleashing the Power Within: Your AI Marketing Toolkit

The marketing landscape is evolving at a dizzying pace, and staying ahead of the curve requires embracing the transformative power of AI. No longer a futuristic fantasy, AI-powered tools are now readily available, offering marketers the ability to streamline processes, personalize experiences, and achieve unprecedented levels of efficiency. Let's explore some of the leading players in the AI marketing arena:

1. HubSpot: Your AI-Powered Marketing Orchestrator

HubSpot, a comprehensive marketing, sales, and service platform, has seamlessly integrated AI into its core functionalities, transforming it into a true marketing command center.

- **CRM Superpowers:** HubSpot's AI-powered CRM goes beyond basic contact management, providing intelligent insights into lead behavior and predicting their likelihood of conversion. This empowers sales teams to prioritize high-value leads and personalize their outreach for maximum impact.

- **Marketing Automation on Autopilot:** HubSpot's AI-driven automation engine takes the guesswork out of campaign management. From email marketing and lead nurturing to social media scheduling and content personalization, HubSpot's AI ensures that your marketing efforts are always on point, delivering the right message to the right audience at the right time.

- **Data-Driven Insights at Your Fingertips:** HubSpot's AI-powered analytics dashboard provides a crystal-clear view of your marketing performance. Identify what's working, what needs improvement, and uncover hidden opportunities to optimize your campaigns for maximum ROI.

2. Marketo: The Marketing Automation Maestro with an AI Edge

Marketo, a leader in the marketing automation space, has embraced AI to elevate its capabilities to new heights, empowering marketers to orchestrate sophisticated campaigns that resonate with their target audience.

- **Email Marketing that Hits the Mark:** Marketo's AI-powered email marketing tools go beyond basic segmentation, analyzing vast amounts of data to understand individual preferences and behaviors. This allows you to craft highly personalized email campaigns that deliver the right content at the right time, maximizing engagement and conversions.

- **Lead Nurturing that Converts:** Marketo's AI-driven lead nurturing engine guides prospects through the sales funnel with personalized content and targeted messaging. By understanding each lead's unique needs and pain points, Marketo ensures that your nurturing efforts are always relevant and effective.

- **Customer Engagement that Builds Loyalty:** Marketo's AI-powered customer engagement tools help you build lasting relationships with your customers. From personalized recommendations and loyalty programs to proactive support and tailored communications, Marketo empowers you to create exceptional customer experiences that foster loyalty and drive advocacy.

3. Salesforce Einstein: Your AI-Powered CRM Guru

Salesforce Einstein infuses the world's leading CRM platform with the power of AI, transforming it into an intelligent assistant that empowers sales and marketing teams to achieve unprecedented levels of performance.

- **Predictive Analytics for Proactive Decision-Making:** Einstein's predictive analytics capabilities analyze historical data and identify patterns to predict future outcomes. This allows you to anticipate customer needs, identify sales opportunities before they arise, and make data-driven decisions that drive revenue growth.

- **Personalized Recommendations for Tailored Experiences:** Einstein's AI-powered recommendation engine analyzes customer data to deliver personalized product recommendations, content suggestions, and service offerings. This level of personalization enhances the customer experience, increases engagement, and drives conversions.

- **AI-Powered Insights for Smarter Marketing:** Einstein provides AI-driven insights into your marketing campaigns, helping you understand what's working, what's not, and how to optimize your efforts for maximum impact. From identifying the best channels to reach your target audience to optimizing your messaging for maximum engagement, Einstein empowers

AI-Powered CRM: Where Customer Relationships Reach New Heights

Gone are the days of static spreadsheets and generic outreach. AI-powered CRM systems are here to revolutionize how you manage customer interactions, track sales, and unlock the goldmine of customer data. Let's explore how AI is transforming the very core of CRM:

1. **Predictive Analytics:** The Future is Now - Imagine knowing what your customers want before they even do. AI-powered CRM systems analyze historical data to predict future customer behavior, empowering you to anticipate needs and tailor your marketing strategies with uncanny accuracy.

2. **Lead Scoring:** Prioritize Like a Pro - No more chasing dead-end leads. AI algorithms step in as your secret

weapon, assessing and ranking leads based on their likelihood to convert. Your sales team can then prioritize high-potential prospects and allocate resources with laser focus.

3. **Customer Segmentation:** Divide and Conquer - One size fits all? Definitely not. AI-powered CRMs segment your customers into distinct groups based on their behavior, preferences, and demographics. This granular understanding paves the way for hyper-targeted marketing campaigns that resonate deeply.

4. **Personalized Communication:** The Art of Connection - In today's world, generic messaging just won't cut it. AI-driven CRMs analyze customer interactions and preferences to enable personalized communication that feels authentic and engaging. Say goodbye to mass emails and hello to meaningful conversations.

5. **Sales Forecasting:** Crystal Ball Not Included - Accurate sales forecasting is no longer a guessing game. AI algorithms step in to analyze your sales data and provide forecasts you can rely on. Plan your sales strategies and set realistic goals with newfound confidence.

Content Management System

AI-enhanced Content Management Systems are transforming the way we create, manage, and deliver content. By integrating artificial intelligence, these platforms offer advanced functionalities that streamline workflows and enhance content quality. Here's a closer look at the key AI-powered features revolutionizing CMS:

1. **Content Recommendations:** AI algorithms analyze user data, such as browsing history and past interactions, to recommend personalized content. This personalized approach enhances user experience, boosts engagement, and encourages retention.

2. **Automated Tagging and Categorization:** Managing large volumes of content becomes effortless with AI-powered automated tagging and categorization. These systems analyze content context, identifying relevant keywords and themes to categorize information effectively, making content easily discoverable.

3. **Content Optimization:** AI-driven tools provide data-backed insights to optimize content for better

performance. These tools analyze various factors, including SEO, readability, and user engagement metrics, suggesting improvements to maximize content impact.

4. **Natural Language Processing:** NLP empowers AI-powered CMS platforms to understand and generate human-like text. This technology enables features like automated content creation, grammar and style correction, and even content summarization, significantly reducing manual effort.

5. **Visual Recognition:** AI-powered CMS platforms utilize image recognition algorithms to analyze and categorize visual content. This simplifies multimedia asset management, allowing for efficient tagging, searching, and optimization of images and videos.

Programmatic Advertising and Real-Time Bidding

Programmatic advertising is revolutionizing the advertising landscape by leveraging AI to automate and optimize the process of buying and selling ad space. At the heart of this revolution lies real-time bidding, a dynamic auction system that ensures ads reach the right audience at the optimal moment. Here's how AI is transforming programmatic advertising:

1. **Laser-Focused Audience Targeting:** Gone are the days of generic ad campaigns. AI analyzes massive datasets to identify and target specific audience segments with pinpoint accuracy. By considering demographics, online behavior, interests, and more, AI ensures that ads resonate with the most receptive audience.

2. **Personalized Ad Experiences:** AI takes ad relevance to the next level by tailoring ad creatives to individual users. This personalization, based on user data and preferences, creates a more engaging and impactful ad experience, increasing the likelihood of conversions.

3. **Real-Time Optimization for Maximum ROI:** AI-powered platforms constantly monitor ad performance, analyzing metrics in real-time. This allows for dynamic adjustments to bids, targeting parameters, and even creative elements, ensuring that campaigns are continually optimized for maximum return on investment.

4. **Combatting Ad Fraud with AI:** Ad fraud poses a significant challenge in the digital advertising world. AI algorithms act as vigilant guardians, detecting and preventing fraudulent activities by identifying suspicious patterns and behaviors. This ensures that ad budgets are utilized effectively and not lost to fraudulent impressions or clicks.

5. **Seamless Cross-Channel Campaigns:** Reaching your target audience across multiple channels is now streamlined with AI-powered programmatic platforms. These platforms seamlessly manage and optimize campaigns across various channels, including display, video, social media, and mobile, ensuring a cohesive and far-reaching advertising strategy.

By embracing AI, programmatic advertising offers unprecedented efficiency, precision, and impact, making it an essential strategy for advertisers in today's digital age

AI: Not Just a Buzzword, But a Game Changer - Real-World Success Stories of AI Implementation

The business world is abuzz with talk of AI, but beyond the hype lie tangible results. Forward-thinking companies across industries are harnessing the power of AI tools to streamline operations, personalize customer experiences, and gain a competitive edge. Let's dive into some compelling case studies that showcase the transformative impact of AI implementation:

Case Study 1: HubSpot - Turning Data into Sales Gold with Predictive Lead Scoring

In today's competitive market, efficiently identifying and nurturing high-potential leads is paramount. HubSpot, a leading marketing automation platform, recognized this challenge and tackled it head-on with AI. Their predictive lead scoring feature leverages machine learning to analyze vast amounts of customer data, going beyond basic demographics to uncover hidden patterns and predict the likelihood of conversion.

This empowers businesses to focus their sales and marketing efforts on the leads most likely to convert, maximizing ROI and driving revenue growth. No more wasted resources on dead-end leads – HubSpot's AI-powered solution ensures that every interaction counts.

Case Study 2: Salesforce Einstein - Outsmarting Inventory Headaches with Predictive Analytics

Inventory management can be a delicate balancing act. Too much stock ties up capital, while too little leads to missed sales opportunities. Salesforce Einstein, an AI-powered CRM platform, offers a smarter solution. One retail company, plagued by stockouts and overstock issues, turned to Einstein's predictive analytics for help.

By analyzing historical sales data, customer behavior, and even external factors like seasonality, Einstein accurately predicted future demand. This enabled the company to optimize their inventory levels, ensuring they had the right products in stock at the right time. The result? Increased sales, reduced waste, and happier customers.

Case Study 3: Google Analytics - Unlocking Website Insights with AI-Powered Analysis

Understanding how users interact with your website is crucial for optimizing performance and driving conversions. Google Analytics, a cornerstone of digital marketing, has embraced AI to provide even deeper insights. A travel company struggling to keep up with fluctuating website traffic patterns turned to Google Analytics' AI-powered features for answers.

The automated insights feature quickly identified trends and anomalies in user behavior, revealing previously hidden patterns. Armed with this knowledge, the company could adapt its marketing campaigns, personalize website content, and optimize the user experience in real-time. This data-driven approach led to increased engagement, higher conversion rates, and ultimately, business growth.

Case Study 4: Adobe Sensei - Content Creation and Curation, Supercharged by AI

In the age of content overload, delivering personalized experiences is key to capturing and retaining audience attention. Adobe Sensei, Adobe's AI engine, empowers businesses to do just that. A media company seeking to streamline its content management processes and deliver more personalized experiences turned to Adobe Sensei for a solution.

Sensei's AI-powered features automated tedious tasks like content tagging and categorization, freeing up human teams to focus on strategy and creativity. Furthermore, Sensei's personalized recommendation engine ensured that users were presented with content tailored to their individual interests, leading to a surge in engagement, content consumption, and ad revenue.

The AI Revolution: From Hype to Reality

These case studies demonstrate that AI is not just a futuristic concept, but a powerful tool already driving tangible results for businesses across industries. From optimizing marketing campaigns and streamlining operations to personalizing customer experiences and unlocking data-driven insights, AI is transforming the business landscape. As AI technology continues to evolve, we can expect even more innovative applications and success stories to emerge, solidifying AI's role as a game-changer in the world of business.

Chapter 4: Personalization and Customer Insights

In today's digital landscape, consumers have evolved - they're no longer passive recipients of information but active participants seeking personalized experiences tailored to their individual preferences and needs. This demand for personalization, however, presents a significant challenge for businesses operating with massive amounts of data. Enter Artificial Intelligence, the key to unlocking the power of this data and transforming it into actionable insights.

This chapter delves into the fascinating world of AI and explores its pivotal role in not only enhancing personalization but also in providing a depth of customer insights previously unimaginable. We'll uncover how AI is revolutionizing the way businesses interact with their audiences, fostering deeper connections and exceeding expectations in our increasingly personalized world.

AI for Personalized Marketing: Tailoring Experiences, Exceeding Expectations

In today's digital age, a generic message simply won't cut through the noise. Consumers crave personalized experiences that resonate with their unique preferences and anticipate their needs. This is where Artificial Intelligence emerges as a game-changer for marketers. By harnessing the power of AI, businesses can transform how they understand and interact with their customers, fostering deeper connections and driving impactful results.

Decoding the Customer: Understanding Preferences Through Data

AI thrives on data, and thankfully, today's digital landscape is overflowing with it. From browsing history and purchase behavior to social media interactions and demographic information, AI algorithms can analyze vast datasets from various sources to paint a comprehensive picture of individual customer preferences. By identifying patterns and trends within this data, AI empowers marketers to move beyond broad segmentation and embrace true one-to-one personalization.

Dynamic Content: A Personalized Touch in Real-Time

Imagine a website that adapts its content in real-time to reflect the specific interests of each visitor, or an email marketing campaign that dynamically tailors its messaging based on individual browsing history. This is the power of AI-powered dynamic content personalization. By leveraging AI, marketers can deliver personalized product recommendations, curate tailored email content, and create customized web experiences that resonate with each individual, ensuring that every interaction is relevant, engaging, and impactful.

Predictive Personalization: Anticipating Needs, Delivering Delight

Predictive analytics, fueled by AI, takes personalization a step further by anticipating future customer behavior based on historical data. Imagine a customer browsing for running shoes online. AI algorithms, analyzing their past purchases and browsing patterns, could predict their need for new running socks and proactively recommend relevant options. This ability to anticipate and address customer needs before they even arise elevates the customer experience from satisfactory to delightful, fostering loyalty and driving conversions.

Beyond Personalization: Predictive Analytics and Customer Behavior

The power of AI extends beyond personalized messaging and recommendations. By analyzing customer data, AI algorithms can unlock invaluable insights into customer behavior, enabling businesses to make data-driven decisions that optimize their marketing strategies and maximize their ROI.

Customer Lifetime Value Prediction: Identifying Your Most Valuable Assets

Not all customers are created equal. Some are destined to be loyal brand advocates, driving significant revenue over their lifetime, while others may represent a lower long-term value. AI-powered CLV prediction models analyze customer data to identify those high-value customers, allowing businesses to focus their resources on nurturing these relationships, developing targeted retention strategies, and maximizing their long-term profitability.

Churn Prediction: Uncovering Hidden Signals with AI

Imagine having a crystal ball that reveals which of your customers are contemplating leaving. AI, in many ways, offers this foresight. By delving into vast amounts of customer data – encompassing purchase history, browsing behavior, customer service interactions, and even social media activity – AI algorithms can identify patterns and anomalies that signal a customer's likelihood of churning.

This isn't about simply flagging customers who haven't made a purchase in a while. AI digs deeper, recognizing subtle shifts in engagement, changes in product usage, and even sentiment analysis from customer feedback, to provide a much more nuanced and accurate prediction of churn risk.

Taking Action: Targeted Retention Strategies

The true power of AI-powered churn prediction lies in its ability to empower businesses to take proactive steps to retain at-risk customers. Armed with insights into *why* a customer might be considering leaving, businesses can implement highly targeted retention strategies.

For example, if AI identifies a customer at risk due to a decline in product usage, a personalized email campaign showcasing new features or offering helpful tutorials might re-engage them. Similarly, if a customer's social media activity suggests dissatisfaction, a proactive outreach from customer service could address their concerns and rebuild their loyalty.

Next-Best Action: Guiding Customer Interactions with Intelligence

Beyond churn prediction, AI takes customer engagement a step further with "next-best action" models. These sophisticated algorithms analyze a customer's current behavior, past interactions, and even their predicted future needs to determine the most effective marketing action to take at any given moment.

This could involve:

- **Personalized Product Recommendations:** Suggesting products or services that align with a customer's interests and purchase history, increasing the likelihood of conversion.

- **Timely Discounts and Offers:** Incentivizing a hesitant customer with a well-timed discount or promotion, encouraging them to complete a purchase.

- **Proactive Customer Service:** Identifying customers who might benefit from additional support or guidance and proactively reaching out to help.

By ensuring that every interaction is relevant, timely, and tailored to the individual customer, AI-powered next-best action models transform generic marketing into personalized journeys that resonate with customers, fostering loyalty and driving long-term engagement.

AI is revolutionizing the way businesses approach marketing, shifting the focus from generic campaigns to personalized experiences that resonate with individual customers. By embracing AI-powered tools and strategies, businesses can unlock a deeper understanding of their customers, deliver tailored experiences that foster loyalty, and make data-driven decisions that drive sustainable growth. As AI technology continues to evolve, its impact on the future of personalized marketing is only going to become more profound.

Sharpening the Focus: AI-Powered Segmentation and Targeting for Laser-Focused Marketing

In the past, marketers relied on broad demographic segmentation, grouping customers into large buckets based on age, gender, or location. While this approach had its merits, it often resulted in generic campaigns that failed to resonate with individual customers. Today, AI is ushering in a new era of hyper-personalization, empowering marketers to segment their audiences with unprecedented precision and deliver laser-focused messages that resonate deeply.

Beyond Traditional Segmentation: Unveiling Micro-Segments with AI

Imagine being able to group your customers not just by broad demographics, but by their unique preferences, behaviors, and even their stage in the customer journey. This is the power of AI-powered micro-segmentation. By analyzing vast datasets – encompassing purchase history, browsing patterns, social media activity, and more – AI algorithms can identify subtle patterns and correlations that would be impossible for humans to detect.

These micro-segments, often consisting of smaller groups of highly similar individuals, provide invaluable insights into customer needs and motivations. Armed with this knowledge, marketers can craft highly targeted campaigns that resonate deeply with each micro-segment, maximizing engagement and conversion rates.

Behavioral Targeting: Meeting Customers in the Moment with AI

Imagine a customer browsing your website, their cursor hovering over a particular product category. AI-powered behavioral targeting recognizes this real-time behavior as a signal of intent and instantly personalizes their experience. Perhaps a pop-up appears offering a discount on items in that category, or a personalized recommendation engine suggests related products they might love.

By analyzing real-time actions – website visits, product views, cart additions, and more – AI enables marketers to deliver the right message at the right moment, striking while the iron is hot and capitalizing on fleeting customer interest.

Geotargeting: Location, Location, Location – Personalized by Place

In today's mobile-first world, location data has become an invaluable tool for marketers. AI-powered geotargeting takes this a step further, analyzing a customer's location in real-time to deliver hyper-relevant content and offers.

Imagine a customer walking past one of your brick-and-mortar stores. AI can trigger a push notification on their smartphone, alerting them to a flash sale or a limited time offer available only at that location. This level of personalization, tailored to the customer's immediate context, is incredibly powerful for driving foot traffic and boosting sales.

AI is transforming segmentation and targeting from blunt instruments into precision tools. By leveraging the power of AI to uncover micro-segments, analyze real-time behavior, and personalize based on location, marketers can break free from the limitations of traditional approaches and deliver hyper-personalized experiences that resonate deeply with each individual customer. This level of precision not only enhances the customer experience but also maximizes marketing ROI, ensuring that every message reaches the right audience at the right time.

The Power of Knowing You: How AI Personalization is Transforming Customer Experiences - Case Studies in Action

The days of generic marketing blasts are fading fast. Today, customers crave personalized experiences that cater to their unique needs and preferences. This is where AI steps in, not as a futuristic fantasy, but as a powerful tool already being wielded by industry giants to deliver exceptional customer experiences. Let's delve into some real-world case studies to see AI-powered personalization in action:

Case Study 1: Amazon - The Recommendation Engine That Never Sleeps

Imagine walking into a bookstore where every shelf is curated just for you, filled with books you're guaranteed to love. That's essentially what Amazon has achieved with its

AI-powered recommendation engine. By meticulously analyzing your every click, purchase, and even time spent browsing, Amazon's algorithms build a detailed profile of your interests.

This goes beyond simply recommending similar items to your past purchases. Amazon's AI factors in browsing history, items you've added to your cart but not purchased, and even products that customers with similar tastes have enjoyed. This results in eerily accurate recommendations that appear seamlessly throughout your browsing experience, driving a significant portion of Amazon's sales and solidifying its reputation as a customer-centric powerhouse.

Case Study 2: Netflix - Your Personal Entertainment Concierge

Gone are the days of endlessly scrolling through TV channels or movie listings. Netflix has redefined home entertainment by leveraging AI to curate a personalized viewing experience for each user. By analyzing your viewing history, ratings, and even the time of day you prefer certain genres, Netflix's algorithms become finely tuned to your unique tastes.

This personalized approach extends beyond just suggesting what to watch next. Netflix also uses AI to personalize artwork and trailers, ensuring that you're enticed by visuals that resonate with your preferences. This obsessive focus on personalization has been instrumental in Netflix's meteoric rise, keeping users engaged and coming back for more.

Case Study 3: Spotify - The Soundtrack to Your Life, Personalized

Music is deeply personal, and Spotify understands this better than anyone. Their AI-powered personalization goes beyond simply creating playlists based on your favorite artists or genres. Spotify digs deeper, analyzing your listening habits, the time of day you listen to certain music, and even how your tastes evolve over time.

This results in features like Discover Weekly, a personalized playlist of fresh tracks curated just for you, and Daily Mix, a series of playlists blending your favorites with new discoveries. By constantly learning and adapting to your evolving musical journey, Spotify ensures that you're always discovering new music you'll love, solidifying its position as a leader in the music streaming landscape.

The Future is Personal: AI-Driven Insights for Deeper Connections

These case studies highlight how AI is transforming the customer experience from a one-size-fits-all approach to a personalized journey tailored to individual preferences. By leveraging AI to gather customer insights, predict behavior, and deliver hyper-relevant content and recommendations, businesses can foster deeper connections with their customers, driving loyalty, engagement, and ultimately, business growth. As AI technology continues to evolve, we can expect even more innovative and personalized experiences that cater to our unique needs and desires.

Chapter 5: Content Creation, Curation, and SEO

AI: The Architect of Intelligent Content in the Digital Age

Content remains the bedrock of successful digital marketing, and artificial intelligence is revolutionizing how we create, curate, and optimize content for a world dominated by search engines. Let's explore how AI is transforming content marketing strategies:

AI-Generated Content: From Automation to Amplified Creativity

1. **Automated Content Generation: Scaling Content Creation Efforts:** AI-powered tools, such as the impressive GPT-4, are capable of generating high-quality written content across various formats, including blog posts, articles, product descriptions, and social media updates. These tools analyze vast datasets and contextual information to produce coherent, engaging, and informative content, freeing up marketers from tedious writing tasks and allowing them to focus on strategy and creativity.

2. **Content Templates and Suggestions: Maintaining Consistency and Quality:** AI assists in content creation by providing marketers with templates and suggestions based on best practices and successful content examples. This ensures brand consistency, maintains content quality, and aligns messaging with overall marketing objectives.

3. **Enhanced Creativity: Sparking New Ideas and Approaches:** AI tools can act as creative partners, generating compelling headlines, brainstorming fresh content ideas, and even drafting entire pieces. By analyzing existing content, identifying industry trends, and understanding audience preferences, AI can inspire new creative approaches and enhance the originality of marketing materials.

Content Recommendation Engines: Delivering Personalized Content Experiences

1. **Personalized Content Recommendations: Tailoring Content to Individual Preferences:** AI-powered recommendation engines analyze user behavior, browsing history, and past interactions to deliver personalized content suggestions. This ensures that users are presented with articles, videos, and products that

genuinely align with their interests, leading to higher engagement, conversions, and customer satisfaction.

2. **Content Discovery: Unveiling Hidden Gems and Expanding Horizons:** AI helps users discover relevant and exciting content by analyzing their interactions and preferences. This ensures that users are exposed to a diverse range of content that aligns with their interests, enhancing their overall experience and encouraging them to spend more time engaging with the platform.

3. **Cross-Channel Recommendations: Creating a Seamless and Personalized Journey:** AI-driven content recommendations can be implemented across multiple channels, including websites, email campaigns, and social media platforms. This ensures a consistent and personalized experience for users, regardless of how they choose to interact with the brand.

AI in Search Engine Optimization: Mastering the Art of Visibility

1. **Keyword Research and Optimization: Unlocking the Power of Search:** AI tools analyze vast amounts of search data, identifying high-potential keywords and phrases that are relevant to a brand's target audience. These tools provide insights into keyword performance,

competition, and search volume, enabling marketers to optimize their content for better search engine rankings and increased organic traffic.

2. **Content Optimization: Crafting Content for Both Users and Search Engines:** AI-powered SEO tools analyze content for readability, relevance, and keyword usage. They provide recommendations for improving on-page SEO elements, such as meta tags, headers, and internal links, ensuring that content is optimized for both human readers and search engine algorithms.

3. **Voice Search Optimization: Adapting to the Rise of Voice Assistants:** With the increasing popularity of voice-activated devices, optimizing content for voice search has become crucial. AI tools help identify conversational keywords and phrases that users are likely to speak when using voice search, ensuring that content is discoverable in this growing segment.

4. **Algorithm Updates and Adaptation: Staying Ahead of the SEO Curve:** Search engine algorithms are constantly evolving, and AI helps marketers stay ahead of these changes. AI tools analyze algorithm updates, identify

AI in Action: Real-World Success Stories of Content Transformation

The transformative power of AI in content creation and SEO is no longer a futuristic concept; it's a present-day reality. Let's delve into compelling case studies that showcase how organizations are leveraging AI to achieve remarkable results:

Case Study 1: The Washington Post - AI-Powered Journalism for a Faster, Wider Reach

The Washington Post, a leading name in journalism, employs a sophisticated AI tool called Heliograf to generate news articles and reports. Heliograf analyzes vast datasets, identifies key trends, and extracts relevant information to produce accurate and timely news content. This frees up journalists from routine reporting tasks, allowing them to focus on in-depth investigations, insightful analysis, and compelling storytelling. By automating content generation, The Washington Post has significantly increased its content output, expanded its coverage of local events, and engaged a broader audience

Case Study 2: HubSpot - Personalized Content Experiences Fueled by AI Insights

HubSpot, a renowned marketing automation platform, harnesses the power of AI to elevate its content marketing efforts. By analyzing user behavior, engagement patterns, and content consumption preferences, HubSpot's AI-powered tools provide personalized content recommendations to individual users. This ensures that users are presented with content that aligns with their interests, increasing engagement and driving conversions. Additionally, HubSpot's AI tools offer optimization suggestions, helping marketers refine their content for better search engine rankings and increased organic visibility.

Case Study 3: Grammarly - AI-Powered Writing Assistance for Enhanced Clarity and Impact

Grammarly, a widely adopted writing assistant, leverages AI to empower users to produce high-quality, error-free content. By analyzing text in real-time, Grammarly identifies grammatical errors, suggests stylistic improvements, and provides clarity and engagement recommendations. This AI-powered tool has become an indispensable resource for writers, editors, and marketers, helping them refine their writing, enhance readability, and ensure their message resonates effectively with their target audience.

Embracing the AI-Powered Future of Content

These case studies highlight how AI is revolutionizing content creation, curation, and optimization. By embracing AI-powered tools and technologies, businesses can:

- **Scale Content Production**: Automate content generation for increased volume and efficiency.
- **Personalize Content Experiences:** Deliver tailored content recommendations for enhanced engagement.
- **Optimize Content for Search**: Improve search engine rankings and drive organic traffic.
- **Enhance Content Quality:** Produce error-free, engaging, and impactful content.

As AI technology continues to evolve, its impact on content marketing will only become more profound. By embracing AI's transformative potential, businesses can unlock new levels of content excellence, engage their audiences more effectively, and achieve their marketing goals with greater precision and impact.

Chapter 6: Automation in Advertising, Social Media, and Email Marketing

The Automation Advantage: How AI is Supercharging Digital Marketing

Automation, a cornerstone of AI's impact on digital marketing, is revolutionizing how businesses connect with their audiences. Let's explore how AI-powered automation is transforming key marketing channels, driving efficiency, personalization, and exceptional results:

AI in Pay-Per-Click Campaigns: Precision Targeting and Optimized Spending

AI is reshaping PPC advertising, making it more intelligent, efficient, and cost-effective:

- **Automated Bidding Strategies:** Gone are the days of manual bid adjustments. AI-powered platforms analyze real-time performance data, competitor activity, and market trends to optimize bidding strategies dynamically. This ensures that ads are displayed to the most receptive audiences at the optimal cost, maximizing ROI and minimizing wasted ad spend.

- **Dynamic Ad Creation:** AI takes ad personalization to the next level by generating dynamic ads that adapt in real-time. By analyzing user data, browsing history, and preferences, AI tailors ad content and visuals to create a more engaging and relevant experience, leading to higher click-through rates and conversions.

- **Laser-Focused Audience Targeting:** AI excels at uncovering hidden patterns and insights within vast datasets. By analyzing demographics, online behavior, interests, and purchase history, AI enables marketers to segment audiences with unprecedented precision. This granular targeting ensures that ads reach the most qualified prospects, improving campaign effectiveness and reducing wasted impressions.

- **Data-Driven Performance Optimization:** AI-powered tools provide continuous performance monitoring and analysis, going beyond basic metrics to deliver actionable insights. By identifying trends, patterns, and anomalies, AI helps marketers understand what's working, what's not, and how to optimize campaigns for continuous improvement.

Social Media Domination: AI-Powered Listening, Engagement, and Support

Social media marketing is being redefined by AI's ability to analyze sentiment, automate interactions, and provide real-time insights:

- **Social Listening on Autopilot:** AI-powered tools act as vigilant guardians of your brand's online presence. They monitor social media platforms around the clock, tracking brand mentions, industry trends, competitor activity, and customer sentiment. This real-time intelligence enables businesses to stay ahead of the curve, respond to opportunities swiftly, and mitigate potential crises.

- **Sentiment Analysis: Decoding the Emotions Behind the Words:** AI goes beyond simply tracking mentions; it delves into the emotional nuances of social media conversations. Sentiment analysis tools accurately gauge the positive, negative, or neutral sentiment expressed in posts and comments, providing invaluable insights into customer perceptions, brand loyalty, and potential areas for improvement.

- **Chatbots and Virtual Assistants: Your 24/7 Social Media Team:** AI-powered chatbots and virtual assistants are transforming social media interactions. These intelligent tools provide instant customer support, answer frequently asked questions, guide users through their purchase journey, and even offer personalized recommendations. This enhances the customer experience, builds brand loyalty, and frees up human agents to focus on more complex tasks.

AI-powered automation is no longer a luxury but a necessity for businesses looking to thrive in the digital age. By embracing these transformative technologies, marketers can optimize their campaigns, personalize customer experiences, and achieve unprecedented levels of efficiency and effectiveness across all their digital marketing efforts.

The AI-Powered Inbox: Delivering Email Marketing that Resonates

Email marketing, a cornerstone of digital outreach, is being redefined by AI's ability to personalize messages, optimize delivery, and drive engagement. Let's explore how AI is transforming email campaigns into personalized conversations:

Personalized Email Campaigns: From Generic Blasts to Tailored Conversations

AI empowers marketers to move beyond generic email blasts and create personalized experiences that resonate with individual recipients:

- **Hyper-Personalization for Maximum Impact:** AI analyzes vast amounts of customer data, including browsing history, purchase behavior, demographics, and even social media activity, to craft highly personalized email campaigns. This includes tailoring subject lines to pique interest, customizing content to match individual preferences, and recommending products or services that align with specific needs and desires.

- **Automated Segmentation: Delivering the Right Message to the Right Audience:** AI-powered segmentation tools take the guesswork out of dividing your email list. By analyzing customer data, AI automatically groups recipients based on shared characteristics, behaviors, and preferences. This ensures that each segment receives highly targeted messages that are relevant to their interests, increasing engagement and minimizing the risk of unsubscribes.

- **Optimal Send Times: Reaching the Inbox at the Perfect Moment:** AI eliminates the guesswork of determining the best time to send emails. By analyzing individual recipient behavior, historical data, and even factors like time zones, AI identifies the optimal send times to maximize open rates and engagement. This ensures that your emails reach customers when they are most likely to be receptive to your message.

- **A/B Testing and Optimization: Continuously Refining for Peak Performance:** AI takes the manual labor out of A/B testing, allowing marketers to optimize their email campaigns with unprecedented speed and precision. AI-powered tools automatically test different elements of your emails, such as subject lines, calls to action, content variations, and even send times. By analyzing the results, AI identifies the most effective combinations, allowing you to continuously refine your campaigns for maximum impact.

AI is transforming email marketing from a one-size-fits-all approach to a highly personalized and effective communication channel. By leveraging AI's ability to analyze data, personalize content, and optimize delivery, businesses can create email campaigns that resonate with their audience, build stronger relationships, and drive conversions.

Automation in Action: Real-World Success Stories of AI in Marketing

The transformative power of AI-powered automation isn't just theoretical; it's being demonstrated daily by businesses across industries. Let's delve into some compelling case studies that showcase the tangible benefits of AI in action:

Case Study 1: Google Ads - AI-Powered Precision in Pay-Per-Click

Google Ads, the world's largest online advertising platform, leverages AI to empower businesses of all sizes to maximize their PPC campaign performance:

- **Automated Bidding for Enhanced ROI:** Google's AI-powered bidding strategies analyze vast datasets in real-time, factoring in user behavior, search intent, competitor activity, and countless other variables to optimize bids for maximum return on investment. This allows businesses to reach the most qualified audiences at the optimal cost, driving conversions and minimizing wasted ad spend.

- **Dynamic Ad Creation for Personalized Engagement:** Google Ads utilizes AI to generate dynamic ads that adapt in real-time based on user data and preferences. This ensures that each ad is tailored to the individual viewer, delivering a more relevant and engaging experience that leads to higher click-through rates and conversions.

- **Performance Analysis for Continuous Improvement:** Google Ads provides robust AI-powered analytics tools that go beyond basic metrics to deliver actionable insights. By identifying trends, patterns, and areas for improvement, businesses can continuously optimize their campaigns for maximum effectiveness.

Case Study 2: Coca-Cola - Sentiment Analysis for Brand Reputation Management

Coca-Cola, a global beverage giant, understands the importance of listening to its customers and proactively managing its brand reputation. Here's how they leverage AI-powered sentiment analysis:

- **Real-Time Social Listening:** Coca-Cola utilizes AI tools to monitor social media conversations around the clock, tracking brand mentions, industry trends, and customer sentiment in real-time. This allows them to stay ahead of potential issues, identify emerging opportunities, and engage with their audience proactively.

- **Sentiment-Driven Marketing Strategies:** By analyzing the emotional tone of social media posts and comments, Coca-Cola gains valuable insights into customer perceptions, preferences, and potential areas of concern. This data informs their marketing strategies, allowing them to tailor their messaging, address customer feedback, and strengthen brand loyalty.

Case Study 3: Sephora - AI-Powered Chatbots for Personalized Beauty Advice

Sephora, a leading beauty retailer, enhances its customer experience and drives sales with AI-powered chatbots:

- **Instant Customer Support and Personalized Recommendations:** Sephora's AI-driven chatbots provide instant support on their website and social media platforms, answering frequently asked questions, guiding users through their purchase journey, and offering personalized product recommendations based on individual preferences and needs.

- **Enhanced Customer Engagement and Loyalty:** By providing a seamless and personalized shopping experience, Sephora's chatbots enhance customer satisfaction, build brand loyalty, and drive repeat purchases.

Case Study 4: Netflix - Content Recommendation Engine for Personalized Entertainment

Netflix, the world's leading streaming entertainment service, leverages AI to provide a highly personalized viewing experience:

- **AI-Powered Content Recommendations:** Netflix's recommendation engine analyzes vast amounts of viewing data, including user preferences, watch history, ratings, and even time of day, to suggest content tailored to individual tastes. This personalized approach keeps viewers engaged and coming back for more.

- **Data-Driven Content Acquisition and Production:** Netflix uses AI to analyze viewing patterns and identify content gaps, informing their acquisition and production decisions. This data-driven approach ensures they are investing in content that resonates with their audience.

These case studies highlight the transformative impact of AI-powered automation across various facets of marketing. From optimizing ad campaigns and personalizing customer interactions to managing brand reputation and making data-driven decisions, AI is empowering businesses to achieve unprecedented levels of efficiency, personalization, and effectiveness.

As AI technology continues to evolve, we can expect even more innovative applications in the realm of marketing. The key takeaway is clear: embracing automation is no longer optional; it's essential for businesses that want to thrive in the increasingly competitive and data-driven landscape of modern marketing.

Chapter 7: Data Analytics, Reporting, and Future Trends

Unlocking Data's Potential: How AI is Revolutionizing Marketing Analytics and Insights

In today's data-driven world, the ability to extract actionable insights from vast amounts of information is paramount to success. AI is rapidly transforming the landscape of marketing analytics, empowering businesses to move beyond descriptive reporting and delve into the realm of predictive and prescriptive intelligence. Let's explore how AI is enhancing data analytics and reporting, providing marketers with the tools they need to make smarter decisions and stay ahead of the curve:

AI in Data Analytics and Reporting: From Insights to Foresight

- **Advanced Data Analysis: Unveiling Hidden Patterns and Correlations:** AI-powered analytics tools possess the ability to process massive and complex datasets with remarkable speed and accuracy. This allows them to identify subtle patterns, correlations, and anomalies that might easily escape human analysts. By uncovering these hidden insights, businesses gain a deeper understanding of customer behavior, market trends, and the factors driving campaign performance.

- **Predictive Analytics: Anticipating the Future to Shape Better Outcomes:** AI takes data analysis a step further by enabling predictive modeling. By analyzing historical data and identifying recurring patterns, AI algorithms can forecast future outcomes with remarkable accuracy. This empowers businesses to anticipate customer needs, predict market shifts, and proactively adjust their strategies to capitalize on opportunities and mitigate potential risks.

- **Real-Time Analytics: Agility and Responsiveness in the Moment:** In today's fast-paced digital landscape, the ability to react quickly to changing market conditions and customer behavior is crucial. AI-powered tools provide real-time analytics, delivering up-to-the-minute insights into campaign performance, customer engagement, and market trends. This allows marketers to monitor the effectiveness of their efforts, identify areas for improvement, and make data-driven adjustments on the fly, ensuring that their campaigns remain agile, relevant, and impactful.

- **Automated Reporting: From Manual Tasks to Strategic Focus:** AI streamlines and enhances the often tedious and time-consuming process of generating marketing reports. AI-powered tools can automatically gather data from various sources, analyze it according to predefined parameters, and generate visually compelling reports that highlight key metrics, trends, and insights. This frees up marketers from manual data crunching, allowing them to dedicate more time to strategic planning, creative thinking, and high-level decision-making.

Emerging Trends: Shaping the Future of AI in Marketing

The evolution of AI in marketing is far from over. Here are some emerging trends poised to further revolutionize the industry:

- **Hyper-Personalization at Scale:** AI will enable even more sophisticated personalization, tailoring marketing messages, offers, and experiences to individual customers in real-time based on their unique preferences, behaviors, and needs.

- **AI-Powered Content Creation:** AI is already being used to generate basic marketing copy, but its capabilities are rapidly advancing. In the future, we can expect AI to play a larger role in content creation, from writing blog posts and social media updates to even generating video scripts and personalized email campaigns.

- **Voice and Visual Search Optimization:** As voice assistants and visual search technologies become increasingly prevalent, AI will be essential for optimizing marketing content to be discoverable through these new channels.

- **The Rise of AI-Powered Marketing Platforms:** We're seeing the emergence of all-in-one AI marketing platforms that integrate various tools and functionalities, providing businesses with a centralized hub for managing their data, automating tasks, and optimizing campaigns across multiple channels.

AI is fundamentally changing how businesses approach marketing analytics and reporting. By harnessing the power of AI, marketers can unlock the true potential of their data, gain deeper insights, make more informed decisions, and drive exceptional results in an increasingly competitive

Unlocking Data's Potential: How AI is Revolutionizing Marketing Analytics and Insights

In today's data-driven world, the ability to extract actionable insights from vast amounts of information is paramount to success. AI is rapidly transforming the landscape of marketing analytics, empowering businesses to move beyond descriptive reporting and delve into the realm of predictive and prescriptive intelligence. Let's explore how AI is enhancing data analytics and reporting, providing marketers with the tools they need to make smarter decisions and stay ahead of the curve:

AI in Data Analytics and Reporting: From Insights to Foresight

- **Advanced Data Analysis: Unveiling Hidden Patterns and Correlations:** AI-powered analytics tools possess the ability to process massive and complex datasets with remarkable speed and accuracy. This allows them to identify subtle patterns, correlations, and anomalies that might easily escape human analysts. By uncovering these hidden insights, businesses gain a deeper understanding of customer behavior, market trends, and the factors driving campaign performance.

- **Predictive Analytics: Anticipating the Future to Shape Better Outcomes:** AI takes data analysis a step further by enabling predictive modeling. By analyzing historical data and identifying recurring patterns, AI algorithms can forecast future outcomes with remarkable accuracy. This empowers businesses to anticipate customer needs, predict market shifts, and proactively adjust their strategies to capitalize on opportunities and mitigate potential risks.

- **Real-Time Analytics: Agility and Responsiveness in the Moment:** In today's fast-paced digital landscape, the ability to react quickly to changing market conditions and customer behavior is crucial. AI-powered tools provide real-time analytics, delivering up-to-the-minute insights into campaign performance, customer engagement, and market trends. This allows marketers to monitor the effectiveness of their efforts, identify areas for improvement, and make data-driven adjustments on the fly, ensuring that their campaigns remain agile, relevant, and impactful.

- **Automated Reporting: From Manual Tasks to Strategic Focus:** AI streamlines and enhances the often tedious and time-consuming process of generating marketing reports. AI-powered tools can automatically gather data from various sources, analyze it according to predefined parameters, and generate visually compelling reports that highlight key metrics, trends, and insights. This frees up marketers from manual data crunching, allowing them to dedicate more time to strategic planning, creative thinking, and high-level decision-making.

Visualization and Dashboards: Bringing Data to Life

The power of AI in marketing analytics extends beyond raw data processing; it's about transforming complex information into clear, actionable insights. This is where data visualization and AI-powered dashboards come into play:

- **Interactive Dashboards: A Panoramic View at Your Fingertips:** AI-powered dashboards provide marketers with intuitive and customizable interfaces to explore their data visually. These dynamic dashboards go beyond static charts and graphs, offering interactive elements, drill-down capabilities, and real-time data updates. Marketers can easily tailor the displayed metrics and visualizations to focus on the insights most relevant to their immediate needs and goals.

- **Data Visualization: Unveiling the Stories Within the Numbers:** AI tools excel at transforming raw data into compelling visual representations that are easy to understand and interpret. By leveraging various chart types, graphs, heatmaps, and even geographical maps, AI helps marketers identify trends, patterns, and outliers that might otherwise remain hidden in spreadsheets. This visual approach makes it significantly easier to communicate insights to stakeholders, fostering data-driven decision-making across the organization.

- **Anomaly Detection: Proactive Alerts for Opportunities and Risks:** AI algorithms are adept at detecting anomalies—those data points that deviate significantly from the norm. In a marketing context, these anomalies could represent anything from a sudden surge in website traffic to an unexpected drop in conversion rates. By proactively alerting marketers

Gazing into the Crystal Ball: The Future of AI in Digital Marketing

The digital marketing landscape is in constant flux, driven by evolving consumer behaviors and rapid technological advancements. Artificial intelligence is poised to revolutionize the way brands connect with their audiences and navigate the complexities of the digital age. Let's explore some of the most compelling future trends in AI and digital marketing:

1. The Rise of Voice and Conversation: A New Era of Interaction

- **Voice Search Optimization: Speaking the Language of the Future:** With the proliferation of voice assistants like Siri, Alexa, and Google Assistant, voice search is rapidly becoming the preferred method for many consumers to find information and interact with brands online. Marketers need to optimize their websites and content for voice search queries, focusing on natural language processing and long-tail keywords that align with conversational search patterns.

- **Conversational AI: Humanizing the Digital Experience:** Chatbots and virtual assistants powered by AI are transforming customer service and engagement. These intelligent agents can handle a wide range of tasks, from answering frequently asked questions to providing personalized recommendations and resolving customer issues in real-time. As AI technology advances, we can expect even more sophisticated and human-like conversational experiences, blurring the lines between human and machine interaction.

2. Beyond Reality: AR/VR Experiences Reimagine Engagement

- **Immersive Product Demonstrations and Virtual Tours:** Imagine being able to try on clothes virtually without stepping into a fitting room or taking a virtual tour of a hotel room from the comfort of your own home.

AI-powered AR and VR technologies are making these immersive experiences a reality. For marketers, this presents a unique opportunity to showcase products and services in engaging and interactive ways, enhancing customer understanding and driving conversions.

- **Experiential Marketing: Creating Memorable and Shareable Moments:** AR and VR open up exciting possibilities for experiential marketing campaigns. Brands can create interactive games, virtual events, and augmented reality experiences that captivate audiences and leave a lasting impression. These shareable experiences can generate buzz on social media, amplifying brand reach and engagement.

3. Hyper-Personalization: Tailoring Experiences to the Individual

- **Data-Driven Insights for Personalized Journeys:** AI empowers marketers to move beyond basic segmentation and deliver hyper-personalized experiences tailored to individual preferences, behaviors, and needs. By analyzing vast amounts of customer data, AI algorithms can identify patterns and predict future actions, allowing brands to deliver the right message, at the right time, through the right channel.

- **Real-Time Personalization Across Touchpoints:** In today's omnichannel world, consumers expect seamless and consistent experiences across all touchpoints. AI enables real-time personalization, dynamically adjusting content, offers, and recommendations based on a customer's current context, behavior, and past interactions. This level of personalization enhances customer satisfaction, fosters loyalty, and drives business growth.

4. Ethical AI: Building Trust in a Data-Driven World

- **Transparency and Explainability: Earning Customer Trust:** As AI plays an increasingly prominent role in marketing, it's crucial for brands to be transparent about their AI practices. Consumers are more likely to trust brands that are open about how their data is being used and how AI is shaping their experiences. Explainable AI is an emerging field that focuses on making AI algorithms more understandable and interpretable, allowing businesses to provide clear explanations for AI-driven decisions.

- **Fairness and Bias Mitigation: Ensuring Equitable Outcomes:** AI algorithms are only as good as the data they are trained on. If the training data reflects existing biases, the AI system may perpetuate or even amplify those biases

AI Revolutionizing Data Analytics: Case Studies and Future Trends

Artificial intelligence is no longer a futuristic concept; it's actively reshaping the landscape of data analytics, empowering businesses to extract actionable insights and make smarter decisions. Let's explore some compelling case studies that demonstrate the transformative power of AI in data analytics and delve into the emerging trends shaping the future of this dynamic field.

Case Studies: AI in Action

1. IBM Watson Analytics: Democratizing Data Insights

IBM Watson Analytics stands as a prime example of how AI is democratizing data analysis, making it accessible to users without specialized technical expertise. This powerful platform leverages natural language processing, allowing users to interact with data using everyday language. Simply ask a question – "What are the key factors driving customer churn?" – and Watson Analytics will analyze the data, identify patterns, and present the findings in easily digestible visualizations like charts and graphs.

Business Impact:

- Faster, More Intuitive Analysis: No more wrestling with complex spreadsheets or writing lines of code. Watson Analytics empowers users to quickly uncover insights, even from large and complex datasets.

- Data-Driven Decision Making: By making data analysis accessible to a wider audience, Watson Analytics fosters a culture of data-driven decision-making across organizations.

- Enhanced Marketing ROI: Marketing teams can leverage Watson Analytics to analyze campaign performance, identify optimal target audiences, and personalize messaging for greater impact.

2. **Nike: Predicting the Future of Footwear with AI**

Global sportswear giant Nike demonstrates the power of AI-powered predictive analytics in optimizing inventory management and staying ahead of ever-changing consumer demands. By analyzing vast datasets encompassing historical sales figures, seasonal trends, social media sentiment, and even weather patterns, Nike's AI models can forecast demand with remarkable accuracy.

Business Impact:

- Minimized Inventory Costs: Accurate demand forecasting allows Nike to optimize inventory levels, reducing storage costs and minimizing waste associated with unsold products.

- Enhanced Customer Satisfaction: By ensuring that products are readily available when and where customers want them, Nike enhances customer satisfaction and fosters brand loyalty.

- Data-Driven Product Development: Insights gleaned from AI analysis can inform future product development decisions, ensuring Nike stays ahead of emerging trends and caters to evolving consumer preferences.

3. **IKEA: Elevating Customer Experience with AR and AI**

IKEA, renowned for its innovative approach to furniture retail, seamlessly blends augmented reality and AI to create an immersive and personalized customer experience. The IKEA Place app, powered by AR, allows customers to virtually place furniture within their own homes using their smartphones or tablets. This interactive experience provides a realistic preview of how furniture will look and fit, reducing uncertainty and empowering confident purchasing decisions.

Business Impact:

- Increased Customer Engagement: The interactive and personalized nature of the IKEA Place app transforms furniture shopping from a mundane task into an engaging and enjoyable experience.
- Reduced Purchase Anxiety: By visualizing furniture in their own homes, customers can make more informed decisions, minimizing buyer's remorse and reducing costly returns.
- Data-Driven Personalization: AI algorithms analyze customer preferences, purchase history, and browsing behavior to provide personalized product recommendations, further enhancing the shopping experience and driving sales.

Looking Ahead: Emerging Trends in AI and Data Analytics

The field of AI and data analytics is in a constant state of evolution. Here are some key trends poised to shape the future:

- **The Rise of Voice and Conversational Analytics:** As voice search and voice assistants like Alexa and Siri become increasingly integrated into our lives, businesses need to analyze voice data to understand customer intent, sentiment, and preferences. This will enable them to tailor their marketing messages, product offerings, and customer service interactions accordingly. Imagine a future where your voice assistant not only helps you find information but also anticipates your needs and proactively suggests products or services you might be interested in.

- **Hyper-Personalization at Scale:** AI is making it possible to deliver hyper-personalized experiences to individual customers at scale. This means moving beyond generic marketing blasts to crafting highly targeted messages and offers tailored to each customer's unique preferences, behaviors, and even real-time context. Imagine receiving a personalized discount on your favorite coffee order just as you're walking past the coffee shop – that's the power of hyper-personalization.

- **The Ethical Imperative:** As AI plays an increasingly prominent role in data analytics, it's crucial to address the ethical implications. This includes ensuring that AI systems are trained on unbiased data, used responsibly, and do not perpetuate or amplify existing societal biases. Transparency and accountability will be paramount in building trust and ensuring that AI is used for good.

- **The Convergence of AI and IoT:** The Internet of Things is generating massive amounts of data from interconnected devices. Combining this data with AI's analytical capabilities unlocks a wealth of opportunities for businesses. For example, manufacturers can use AI-powered predictive maintenance to anticipate equipment failures before they occur, minimizing downtime and reducing costs.

- **The Rise of Explainable AI:** As AI systems become more complex, understanding the reasoning behind their decisions becomes crucial. Explainable AI aims to make AI models more transparent and interpretable, allowing humans to understand how and why AI systems arrive at their conclusions. This is particularly important in high-stakes domains like healthcare and finance, where understanding the rationale behind AI-driven decisions is essential for building trust and ensuring responsible use.

Embracing the AI-Powered Future of Data Analytics

The convergence of AI and data analytics is transforming the business landscape, empowering organizations to make smarter decisions, optimize operations, and deliver exceptional customer experiences. By embracing these emerging trends and harnessing the power of AI, businesses can gain a competitive edge in the ever-evolving digital economy. The future of data analytics is intelligent, insightful, and driven by the transformative power of AI.

The AI Revolution: Reshaping the Future of Digital Marketing

The integration of artificial intelligence into digital marketing isn't just a passing trend—it's a fundamental shift reshaping how businesses connect with customers, refine their strategies, and measure success. This book has journeyed through the diverse applications of AI in the digital marketing landscape, from unlocking customer insights and delivering personalized experiences to revolutionizing content creation, advertising, and data analysis.

AI's capacity to process massive datasets and extract actionable insights empowers marketers to make smarter decisions, craft highly personalized customer journeys, and automate repetitive tasks. This translates to increased efficiency, smarter resource allocation, and ultimately, a significant boost to your bottom line.

Looking ahead, the future of digital marketing will be intricately intertwined with advancements in AI. Voice search, conversational AI, augmented and virtual reality, hyper-personalization, ethical AI considerations, and the growing network of the Internet of Things are just a glimpse into the trends poised to redefine the industry. Marketers who embrace these advancements and unlock AI's full potential will be the ones leading the charge in an increasingly competitive and dynamic landscape.

However, the evolution of AI necessitates a parallel evolution in our approach to digital marketing. Continuous learning and adaptation are no longer optional; they are essential. Staying ahead of the curve requires staying informed about new AI developments and best practices. By embracing AI and its capabilities, businesses can elevate their marketing efforts beyond simply reaching audiences—they can cultivate stronger, more meaningful relationships with their customers.

In conclusion, AI is a powerful tool capable of revolutionizing digital marketing when wielded effectively. It unlocks unparalleled opportunities for personalization, efficiency, and data-driven decision-making. As we venture further into the future, AI's role in digital marketing will only become more critical. Those who harness its power today will be the architects shaping the future of marketing tomorrow.

Appendices

Appendix A: Glossary of Terms

Artificial Intelligence (AI): The simulation of human intelligence processes by machines, especially computer systems. These processes include learning, reasoning, and self-correction.

Predictive Analytics: The use of data, statistical algorithms, and machine learning techniques to identify the likelihood of future outcomes based on historical data.

Customer Relationship Management (CRM): A technology for managing all of a company's relationships and interactions with current and potential customers.

Search Engine Optimization (SEO): The process of optimizing content and web pages to rank higher in search engine results pages (SERPs) to increase organic (non-paid) traffic.

Pay-Per-Click (PPC): An internet advertising model used to drive traffic to websites, where an advertiser pays a publisher when the ad is clicked.

Natural Language Processing (NLP): A branch of AI that helps computers understand, interpret, and respond to human language in a valuable way.

Content Management System (CMS): Software used to create, manage, and modify digital content.

Sentiment Analysis: The use of NLP, text analysis, and computational linguistics to identify and extract subjective information from source materials.

Augmented Reality (AR): An interactive experience where objects in the real world are enhanced by computer-generated perceptual information.

Virtual Reality (VR): A simulated experience that can be similar to or completely different from the real world, often involving immersive 3D environments.

www.ingramcontent.com/pod-product-compliance
Lightning Source LLC
Chambersburg PA
CBHW071940210526
45479CB00002B/762